My First Christmas

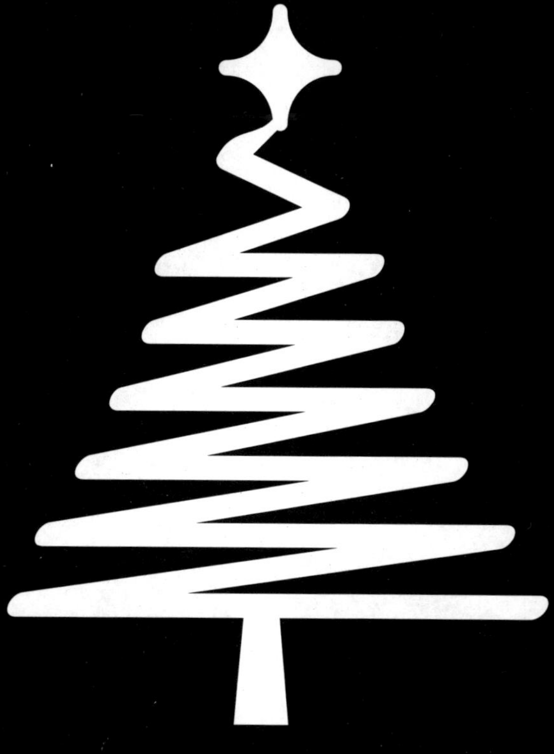

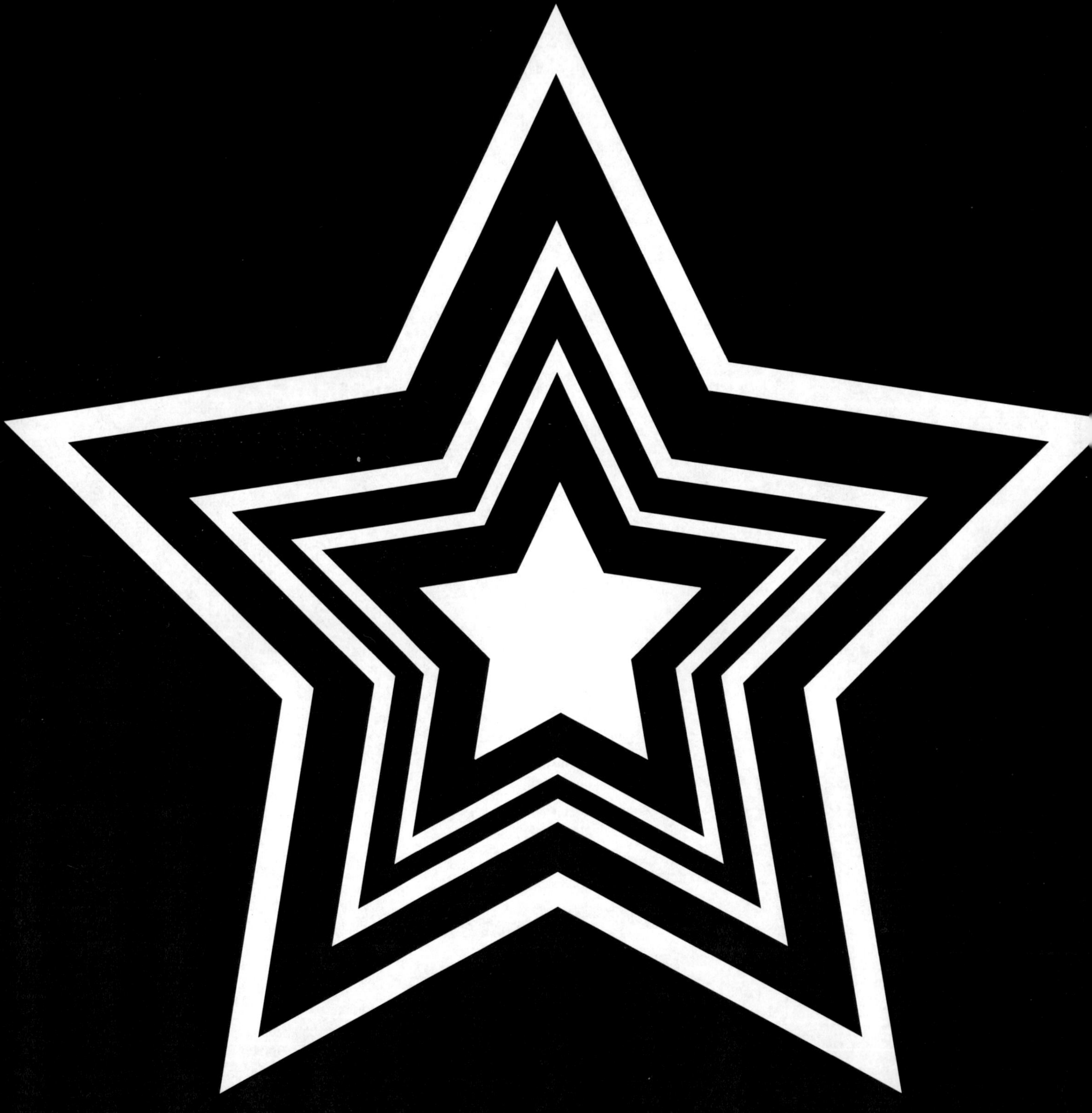

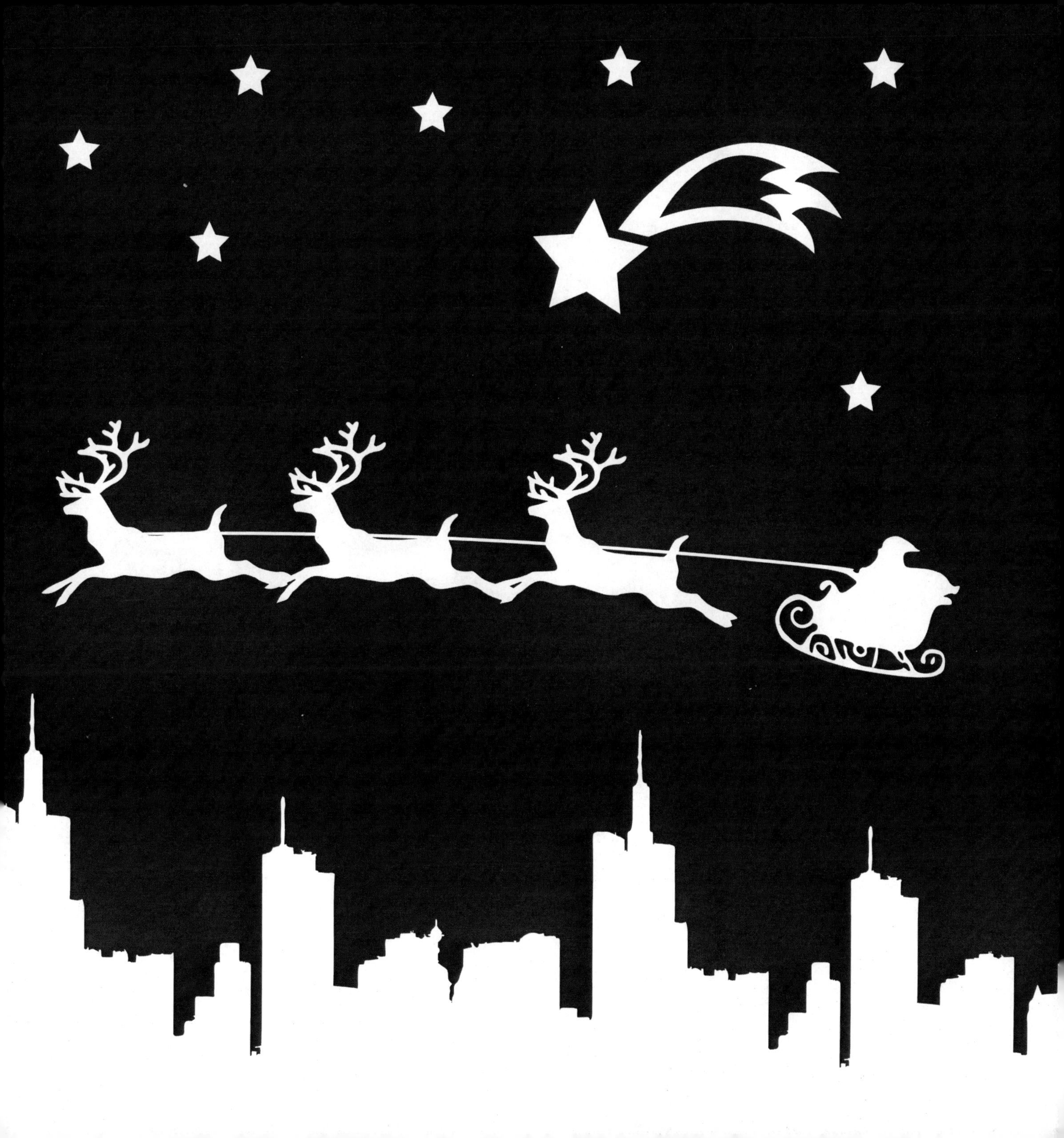

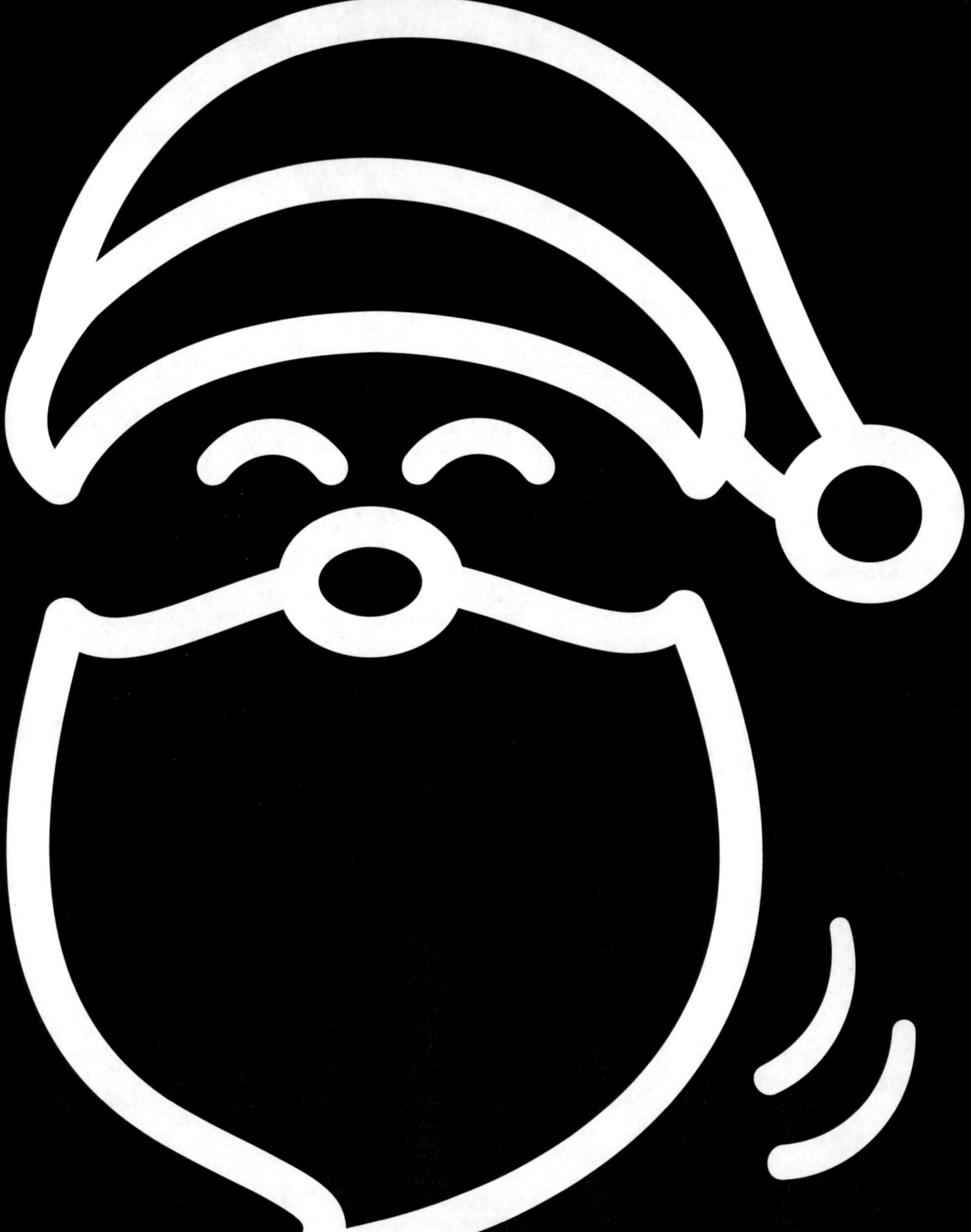

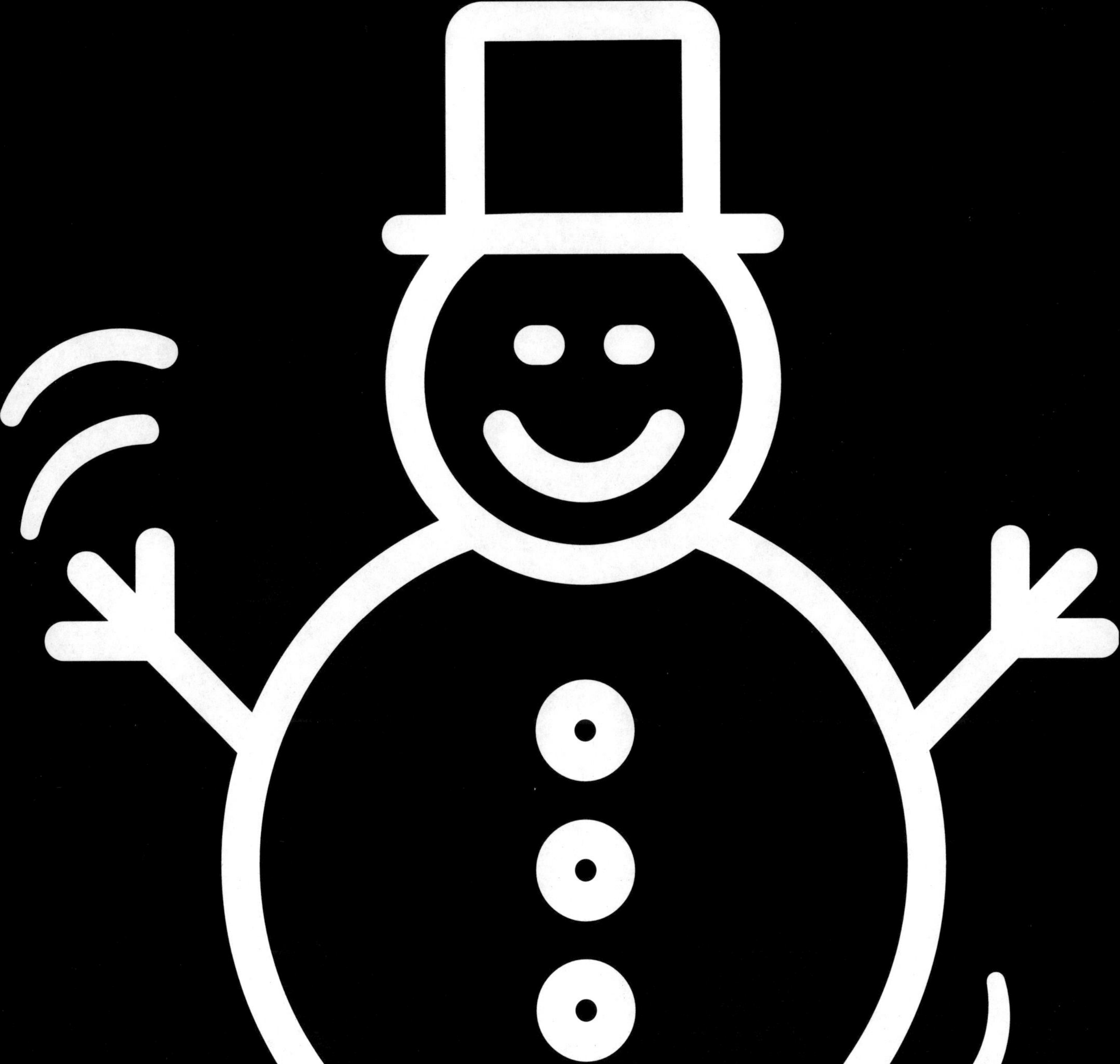

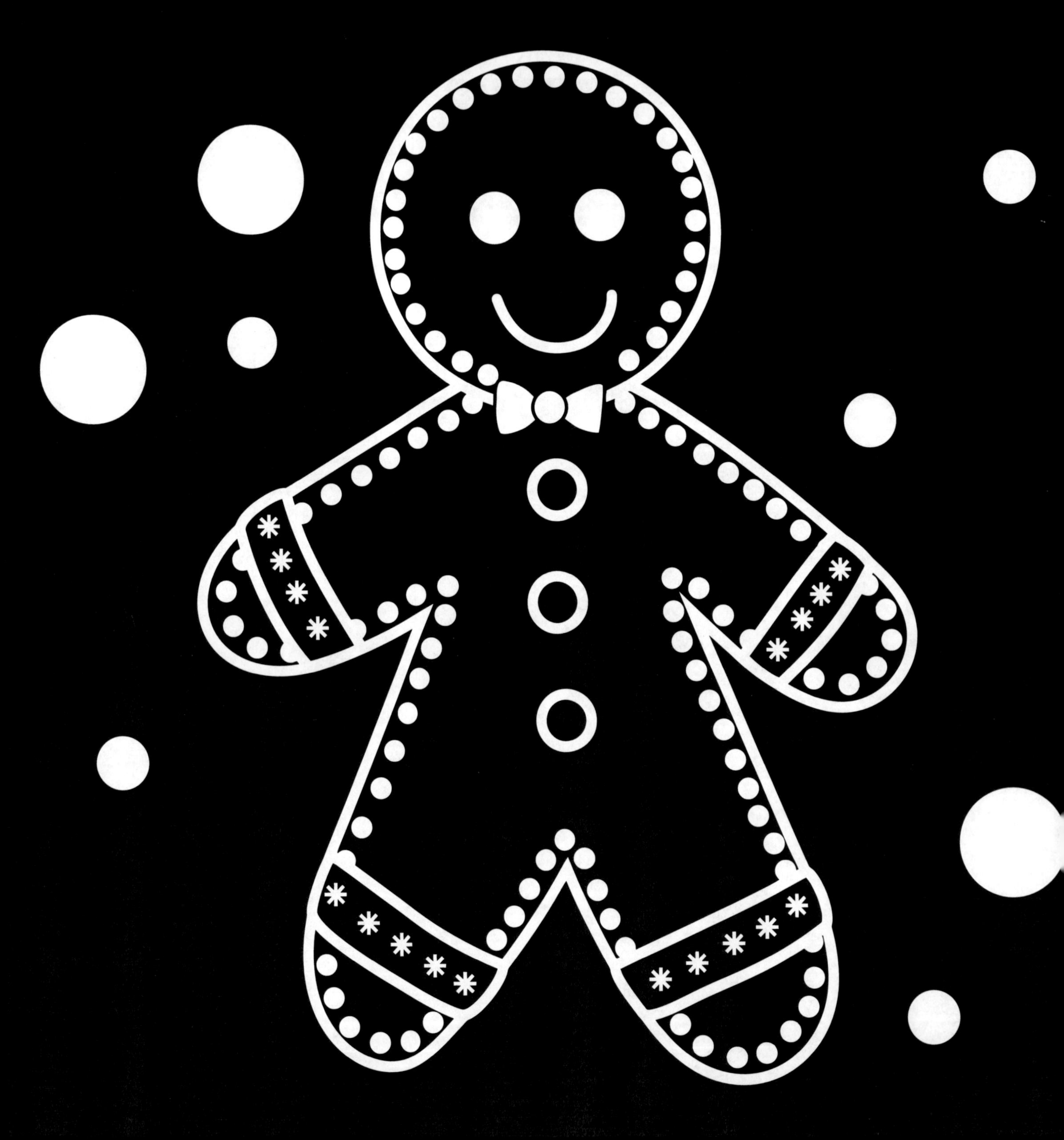

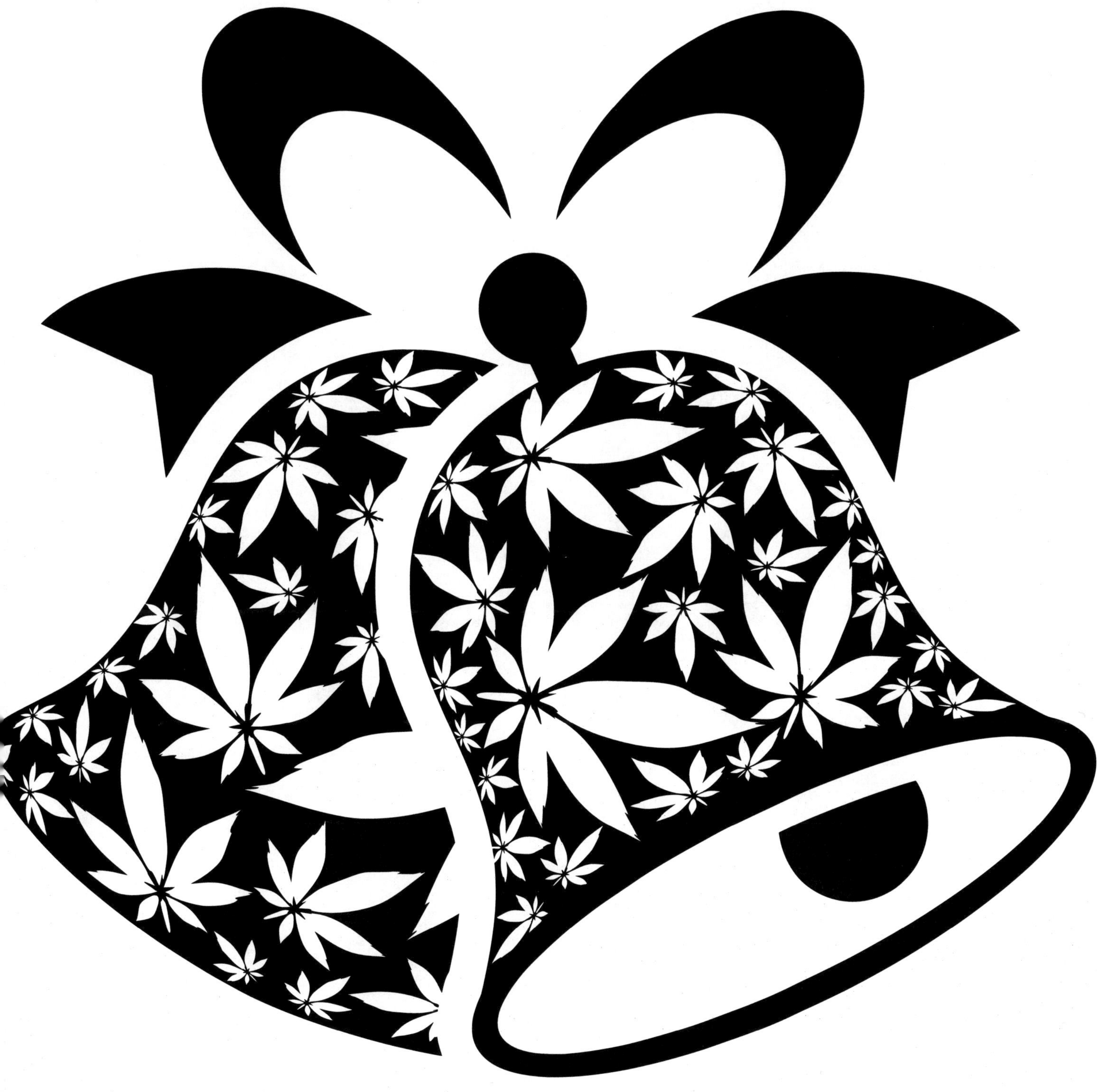

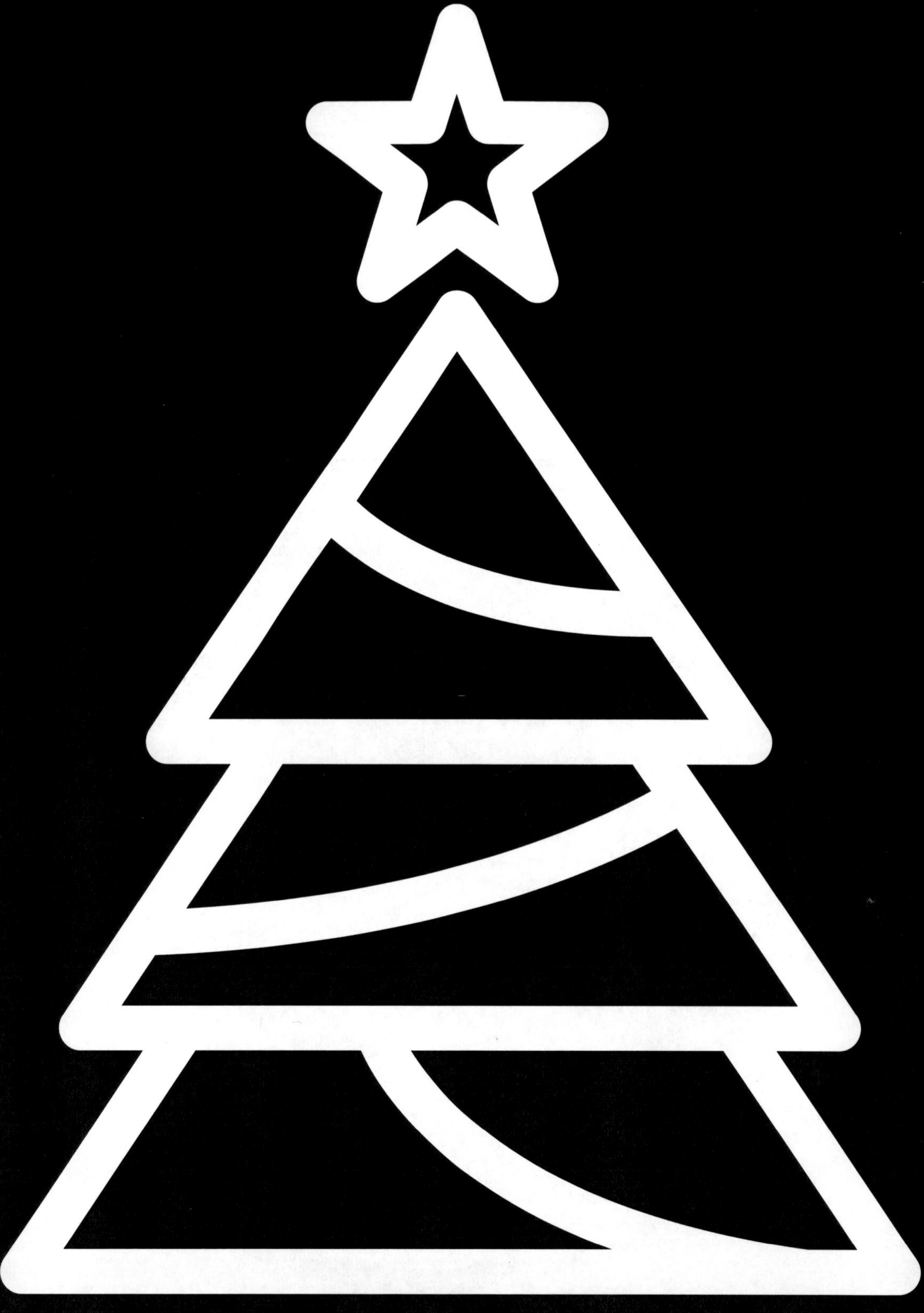

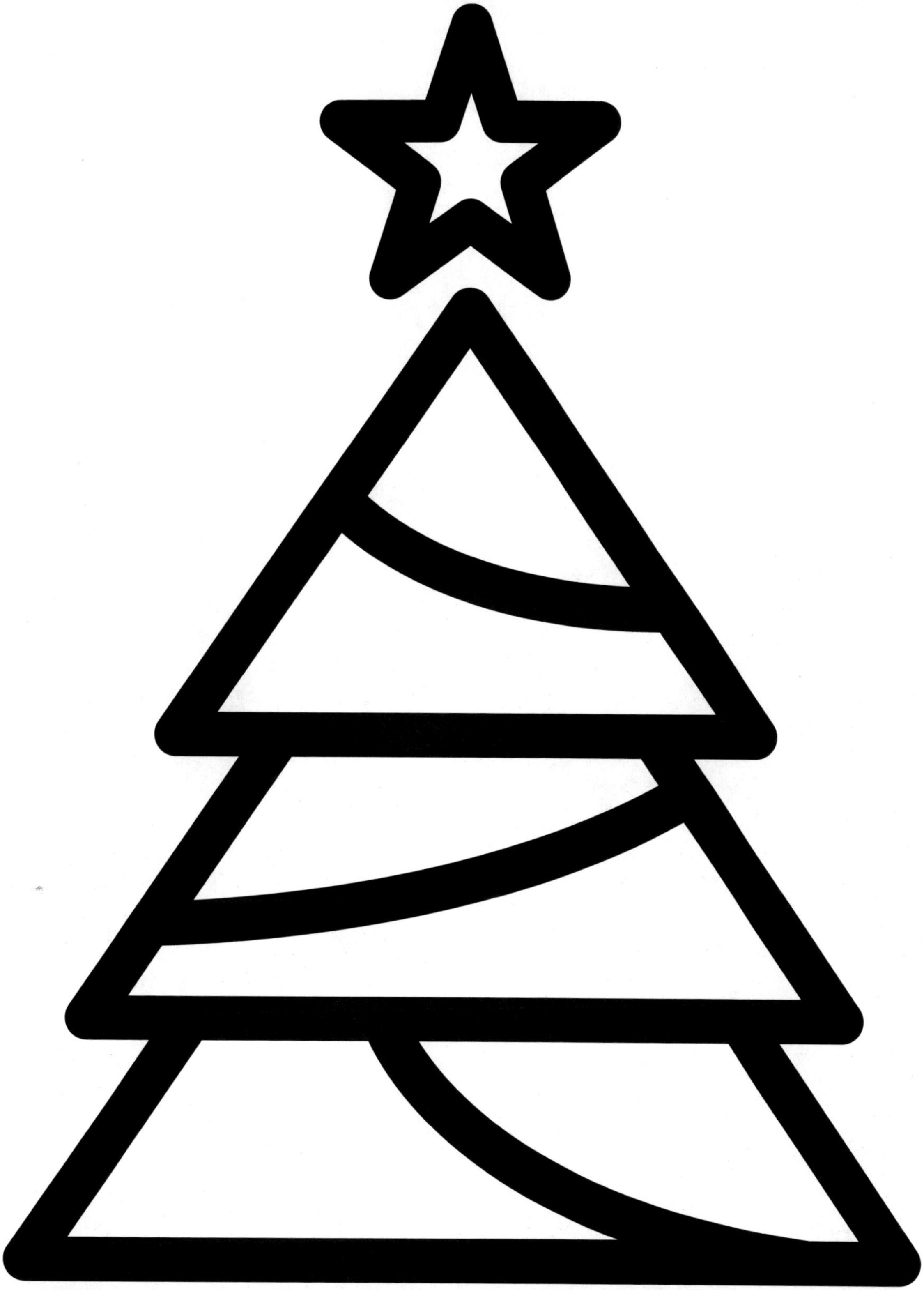

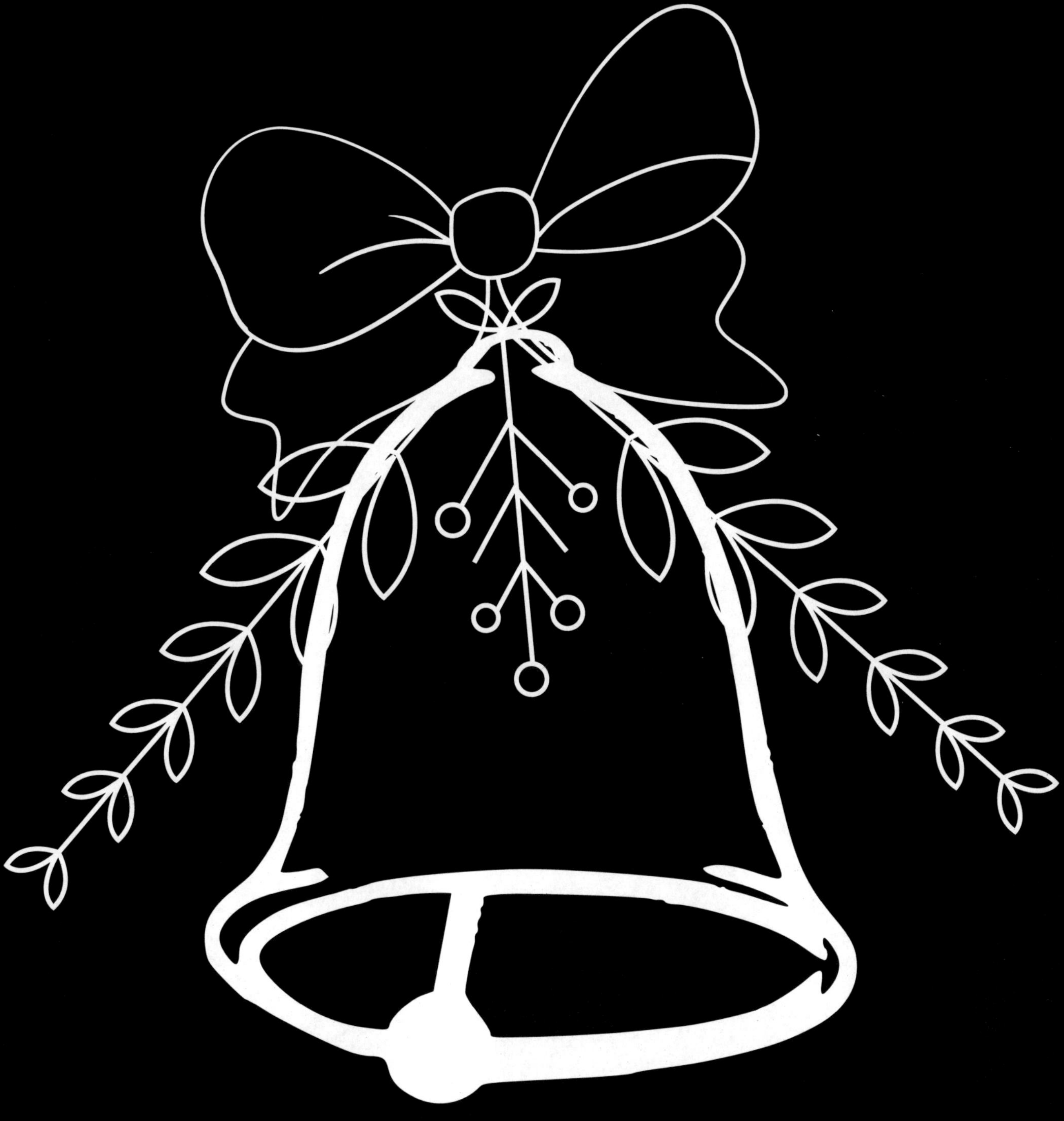

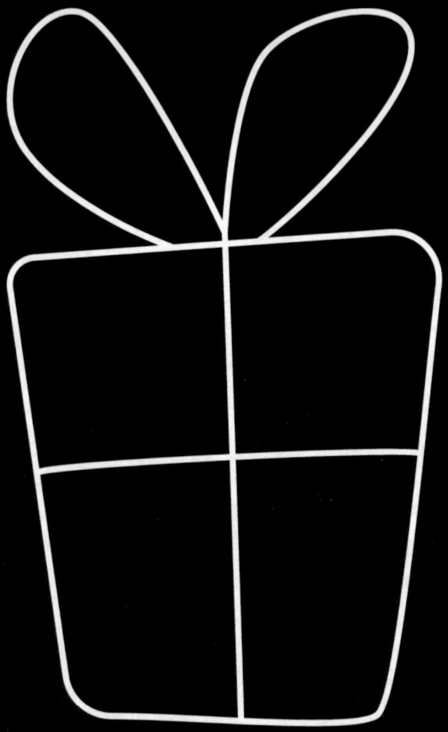
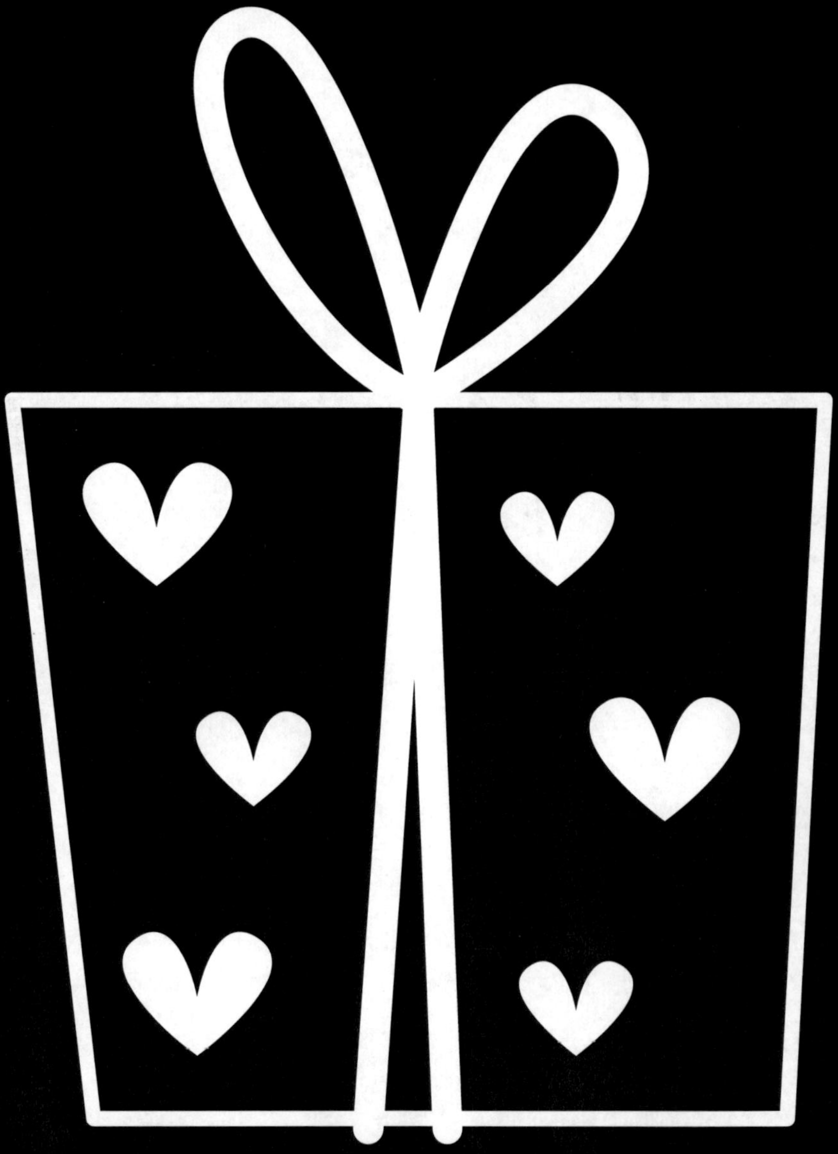

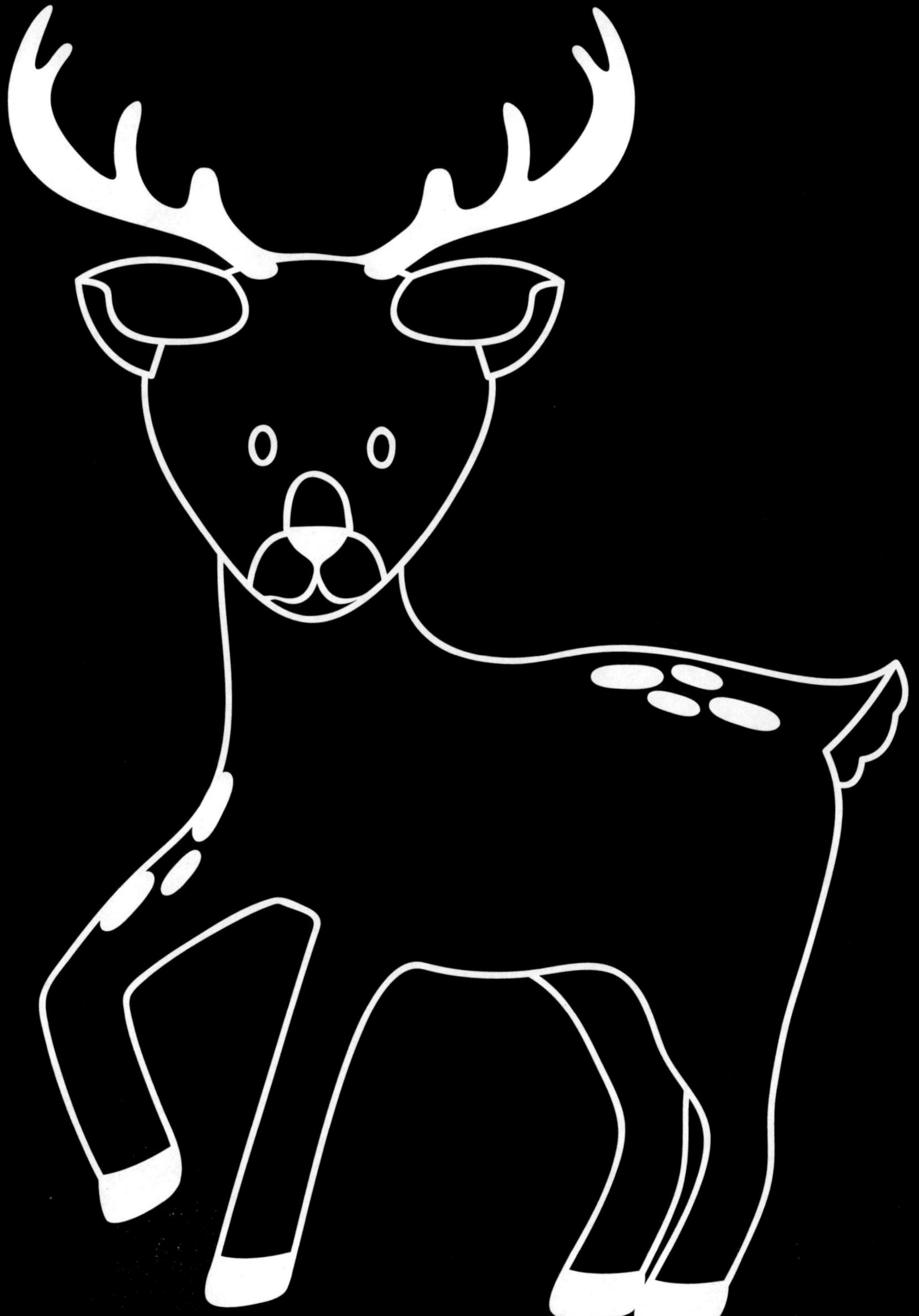

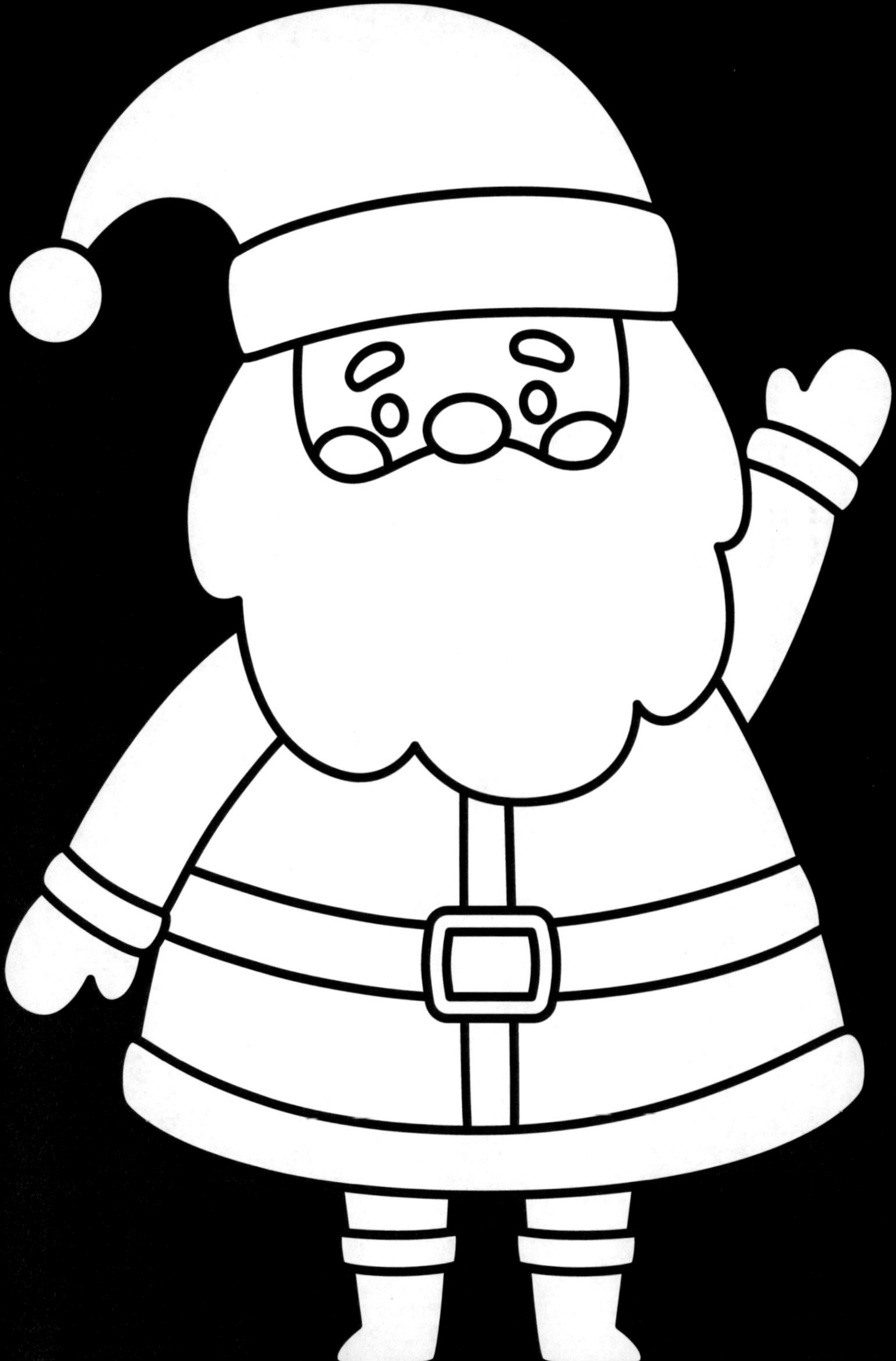

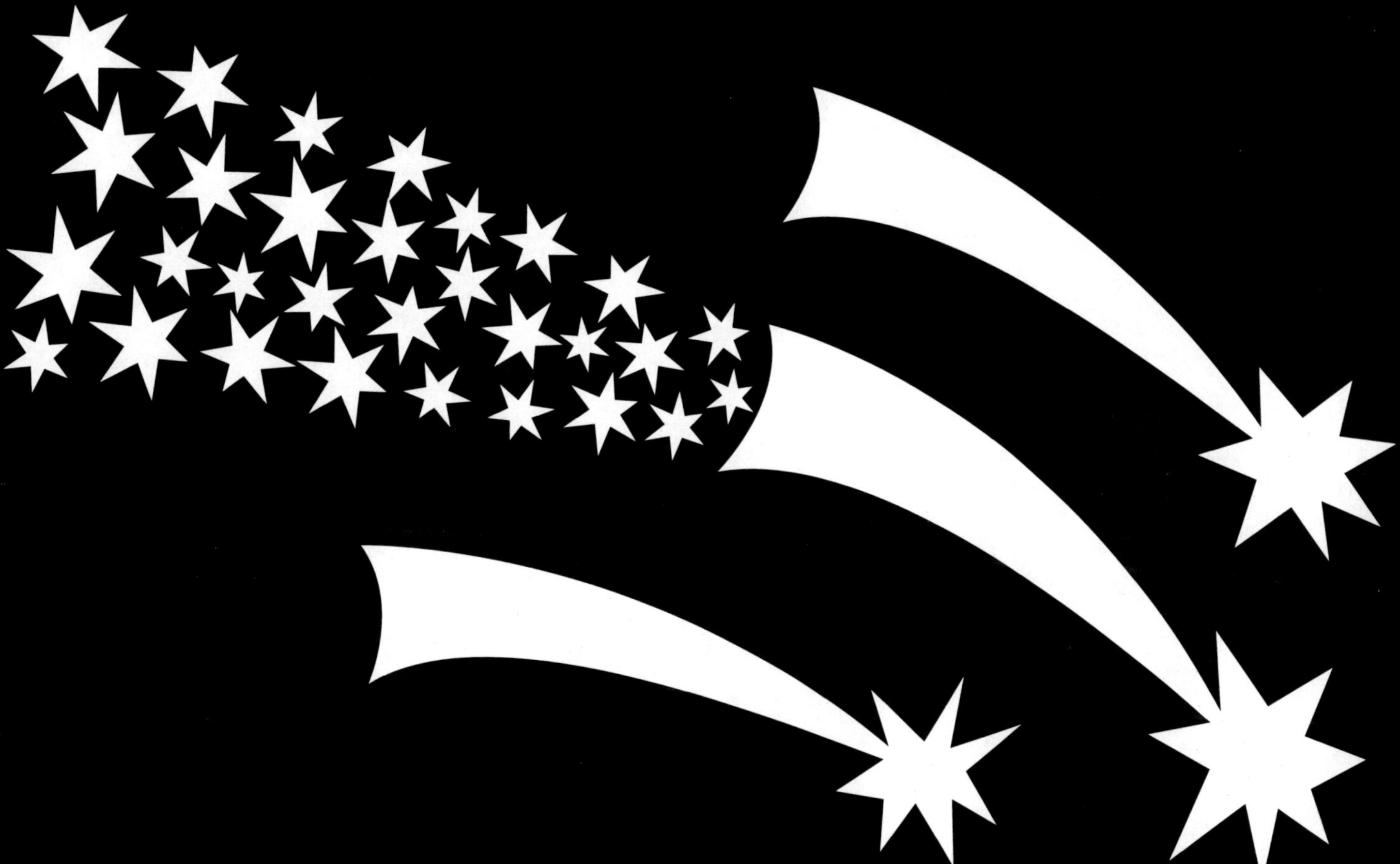

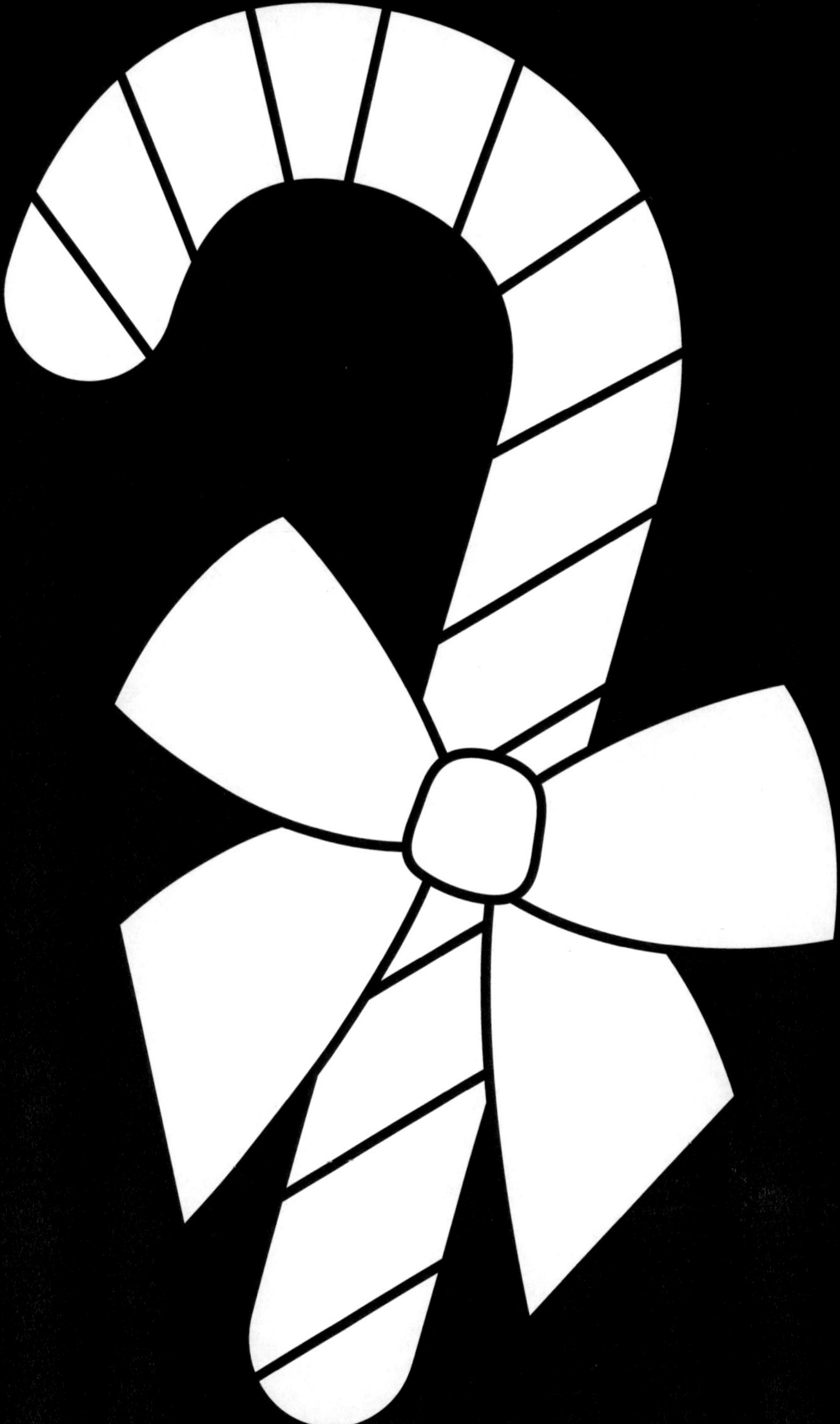

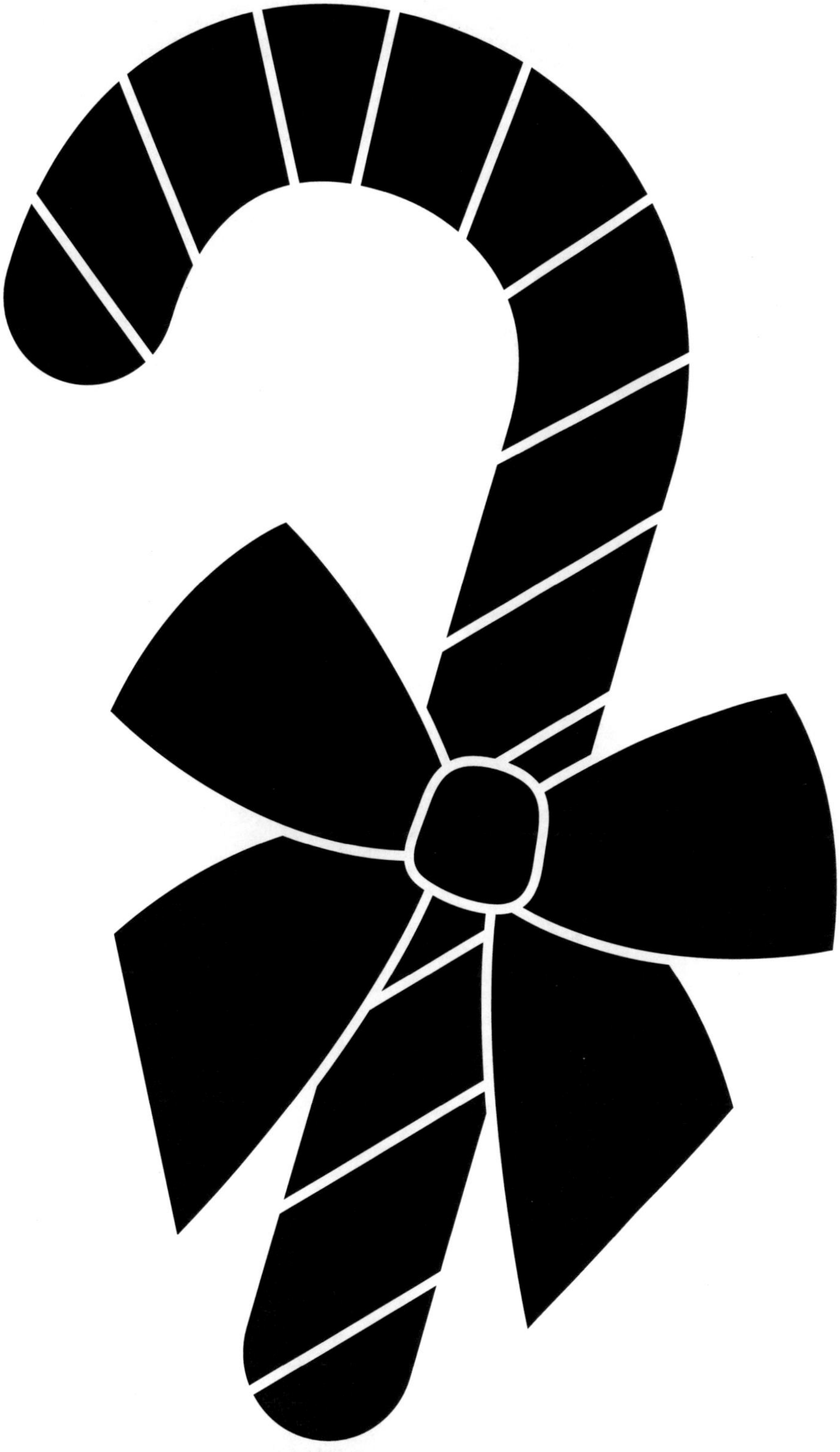

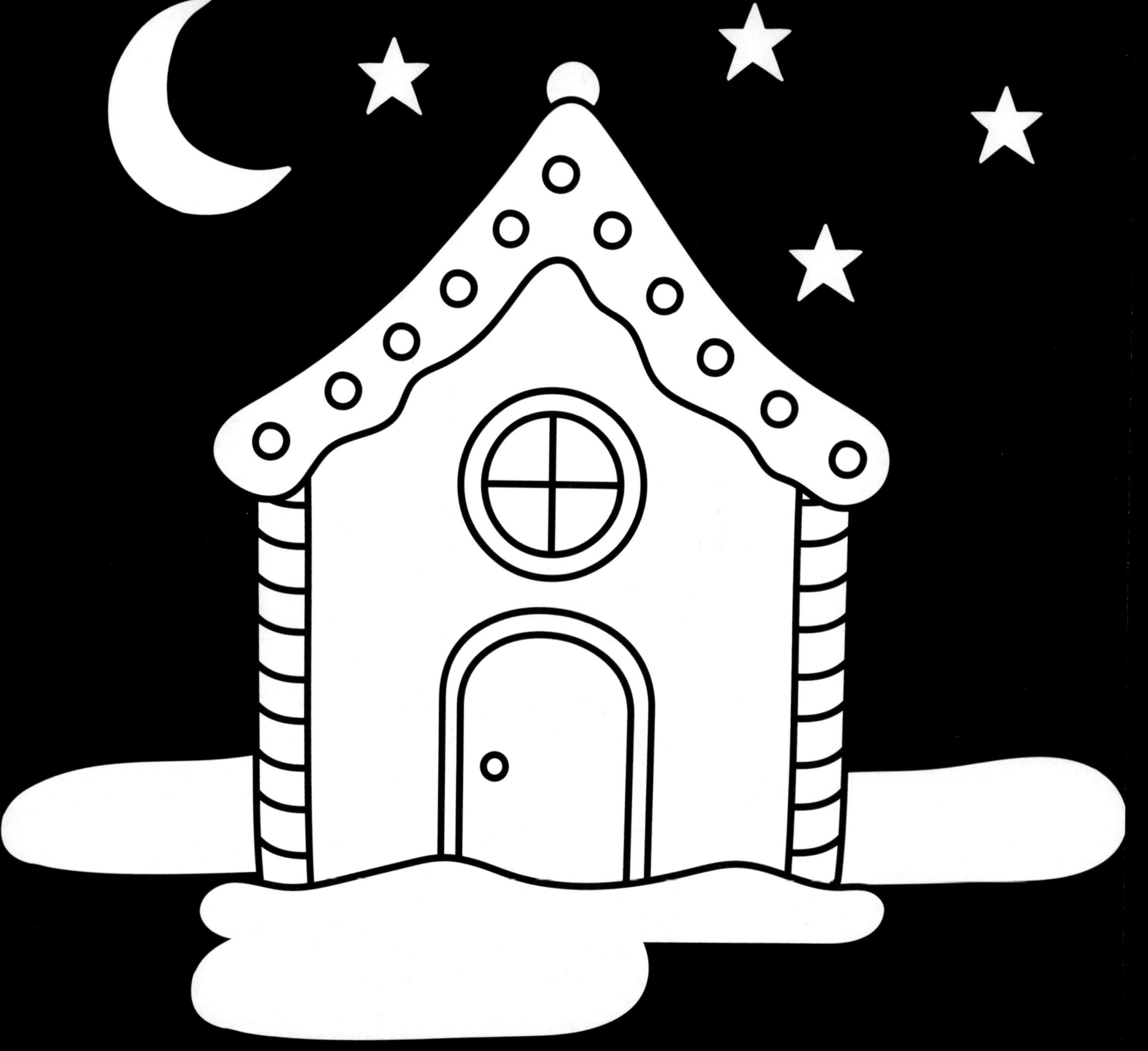

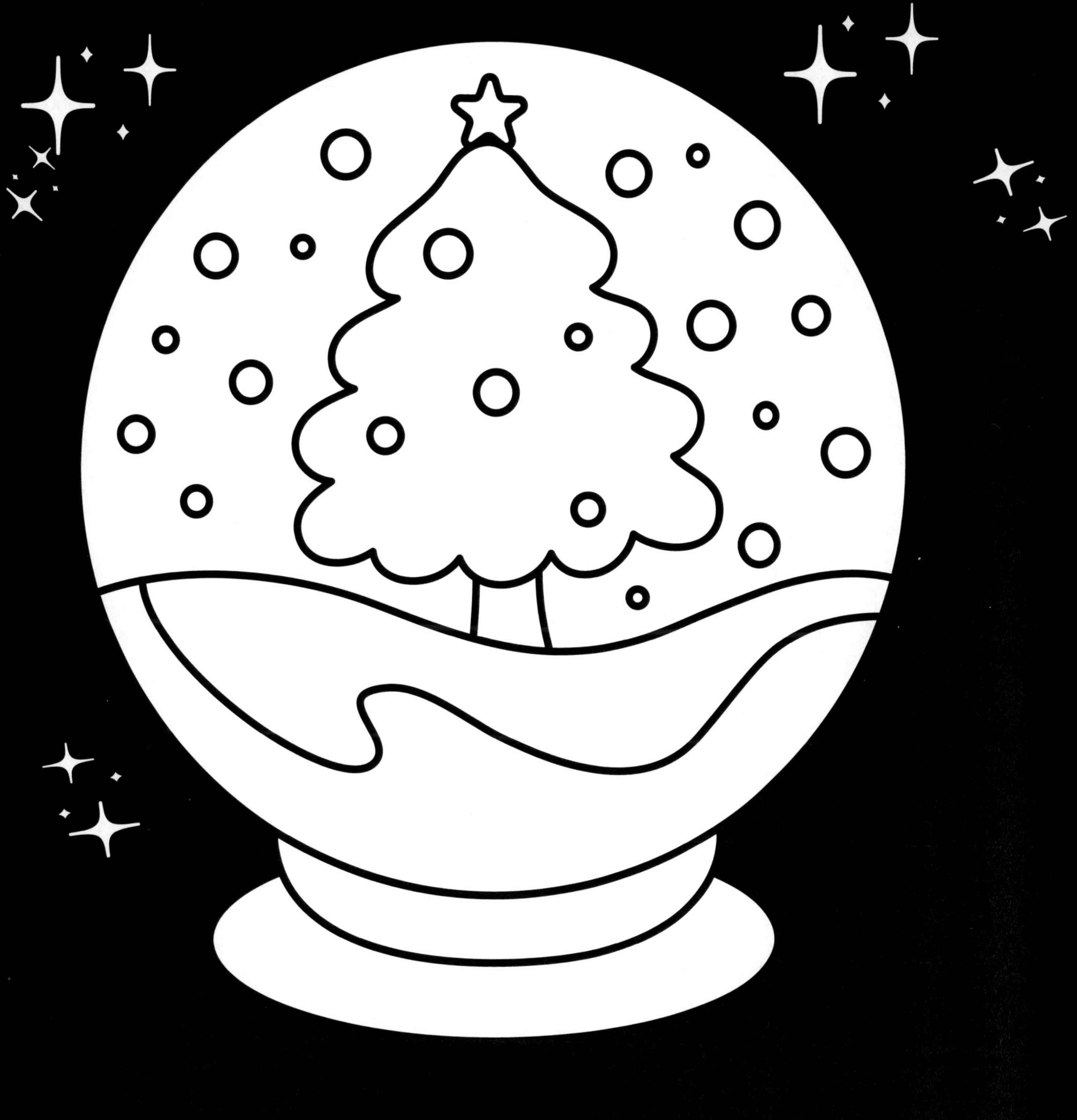

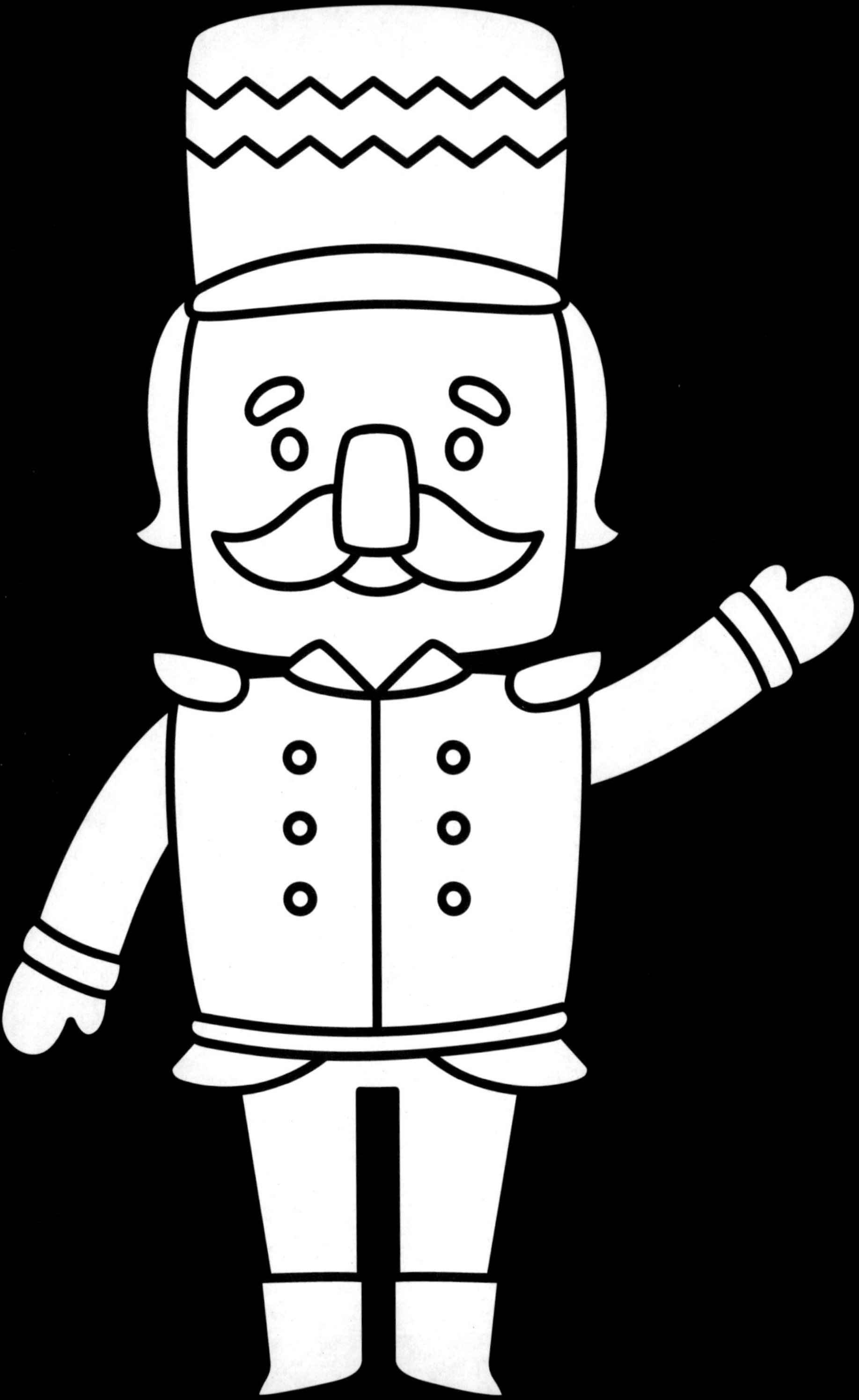

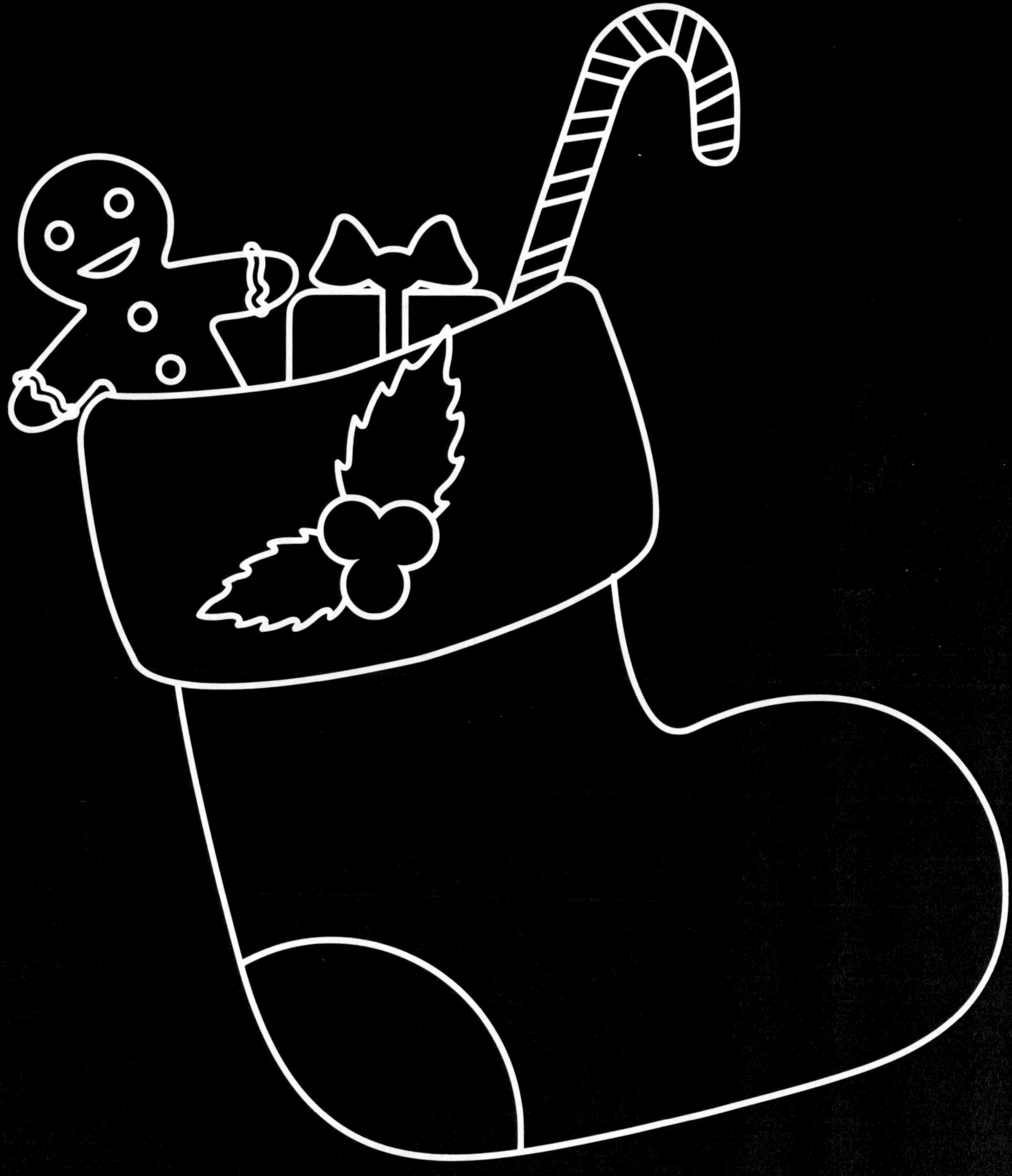

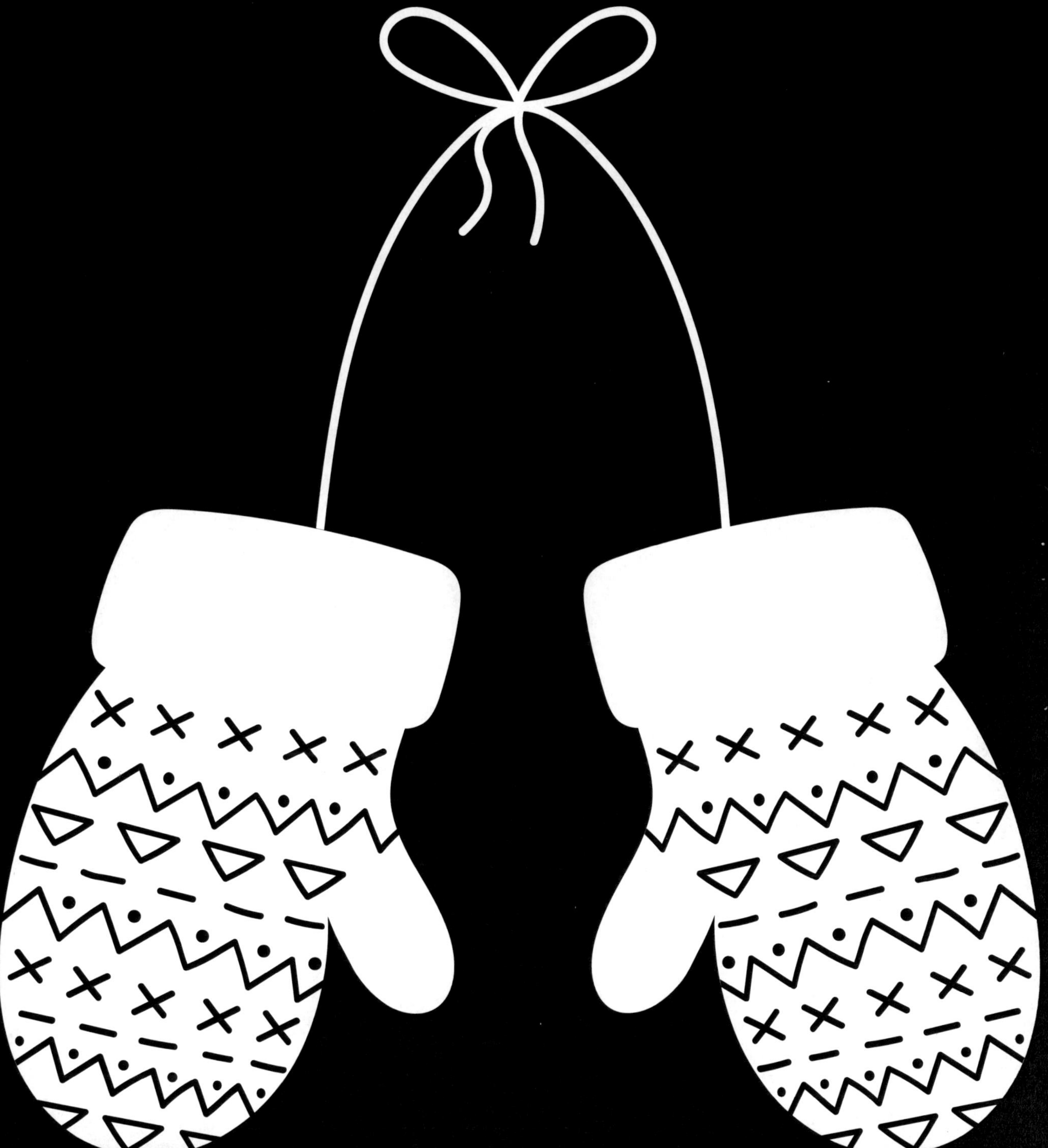

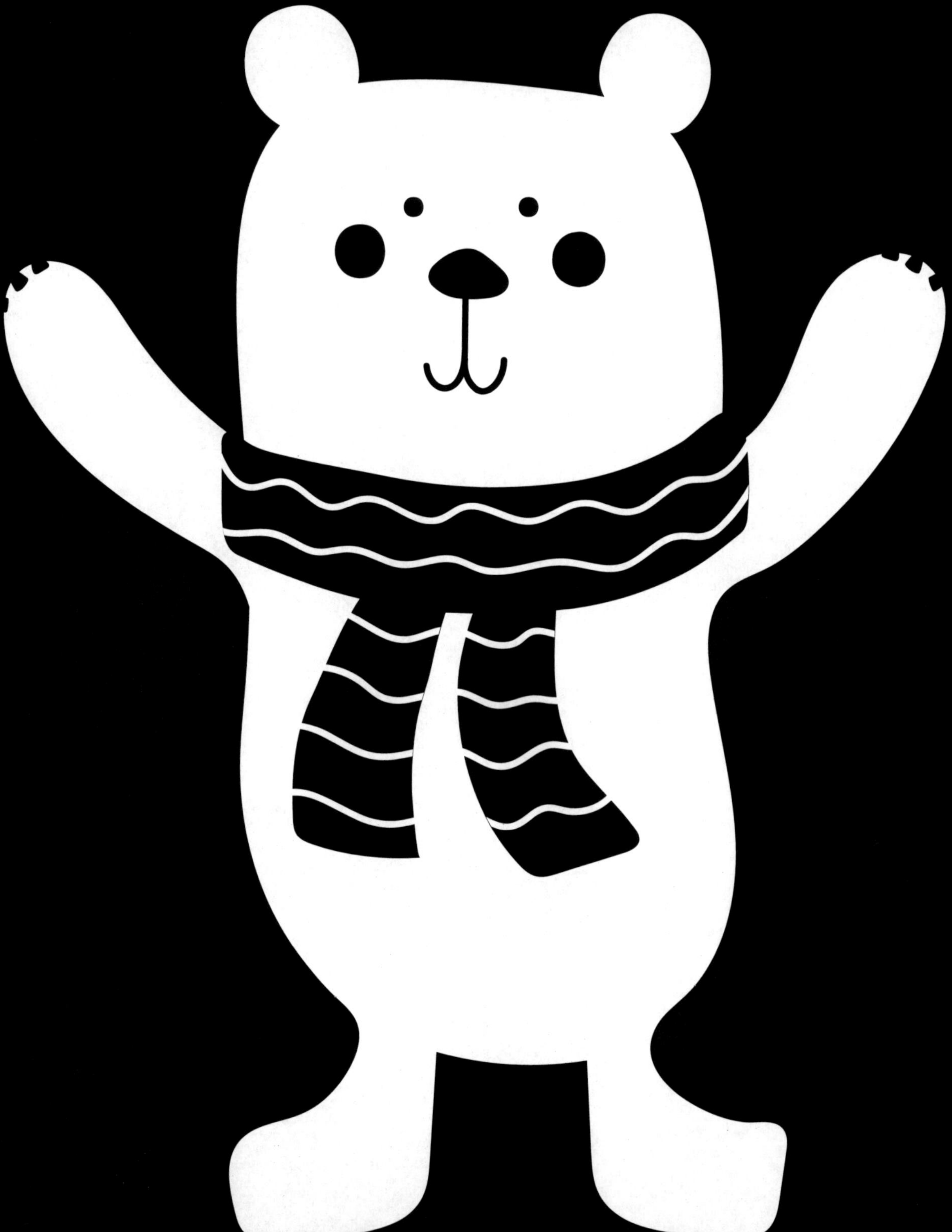

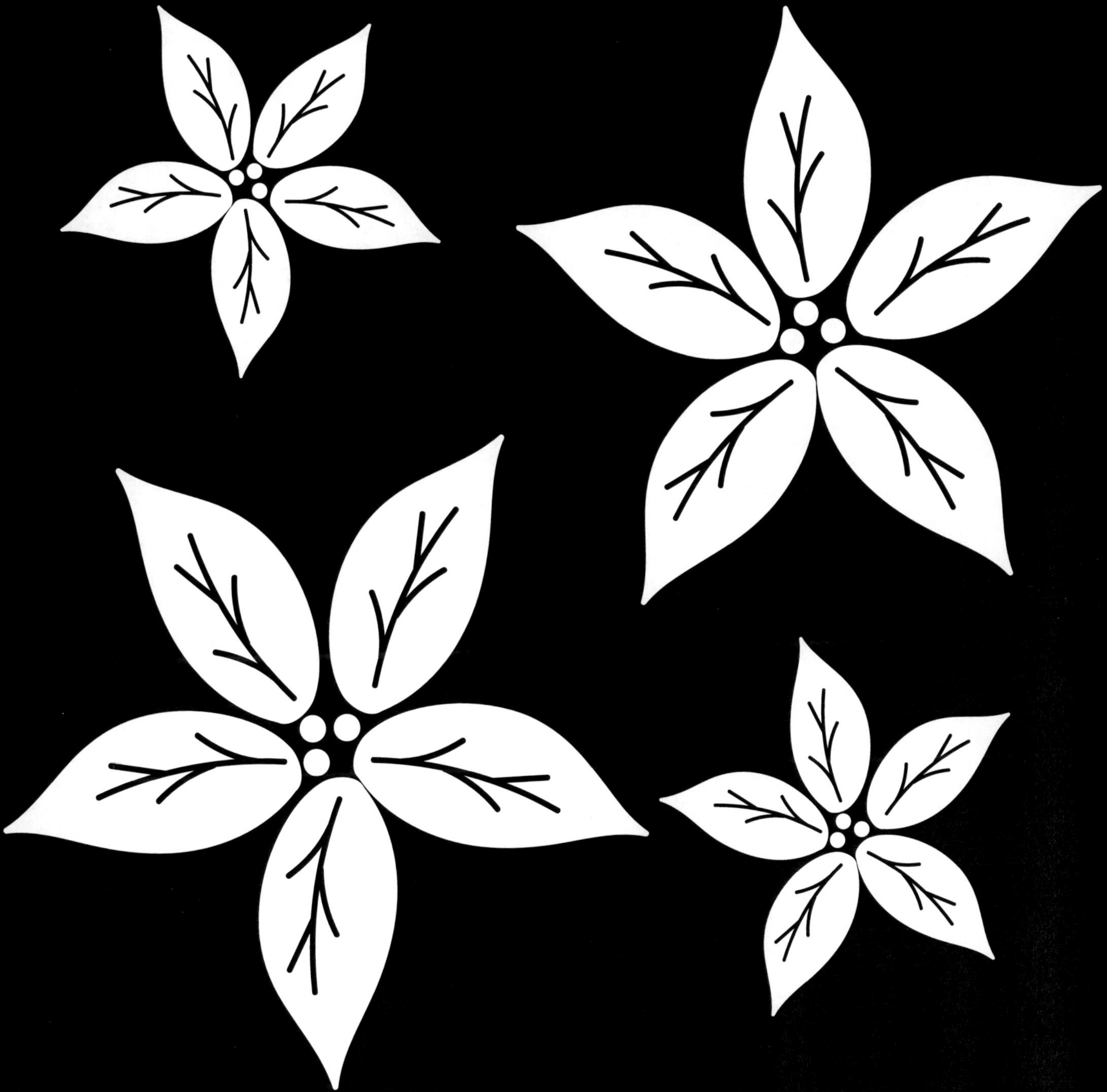

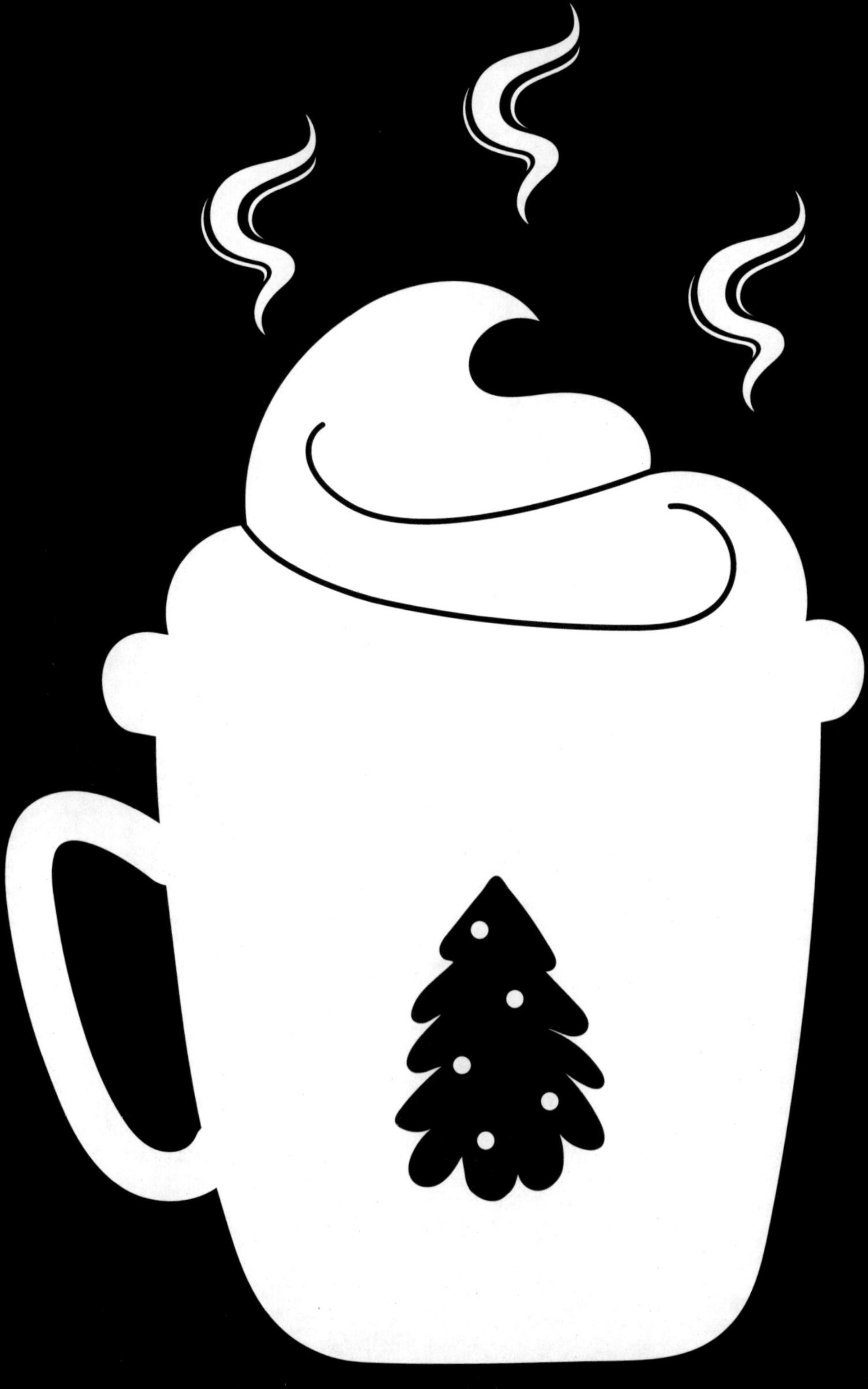

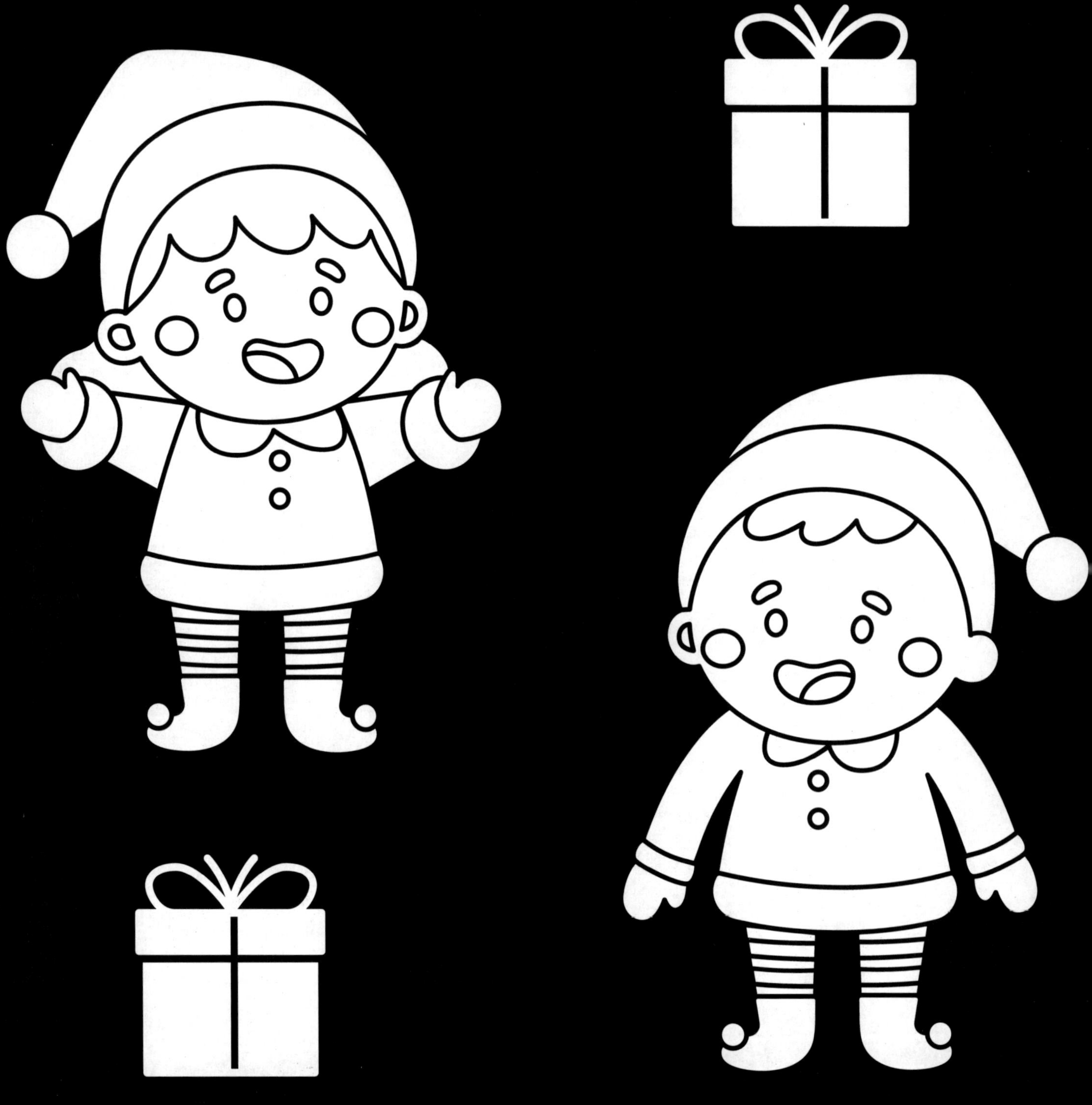

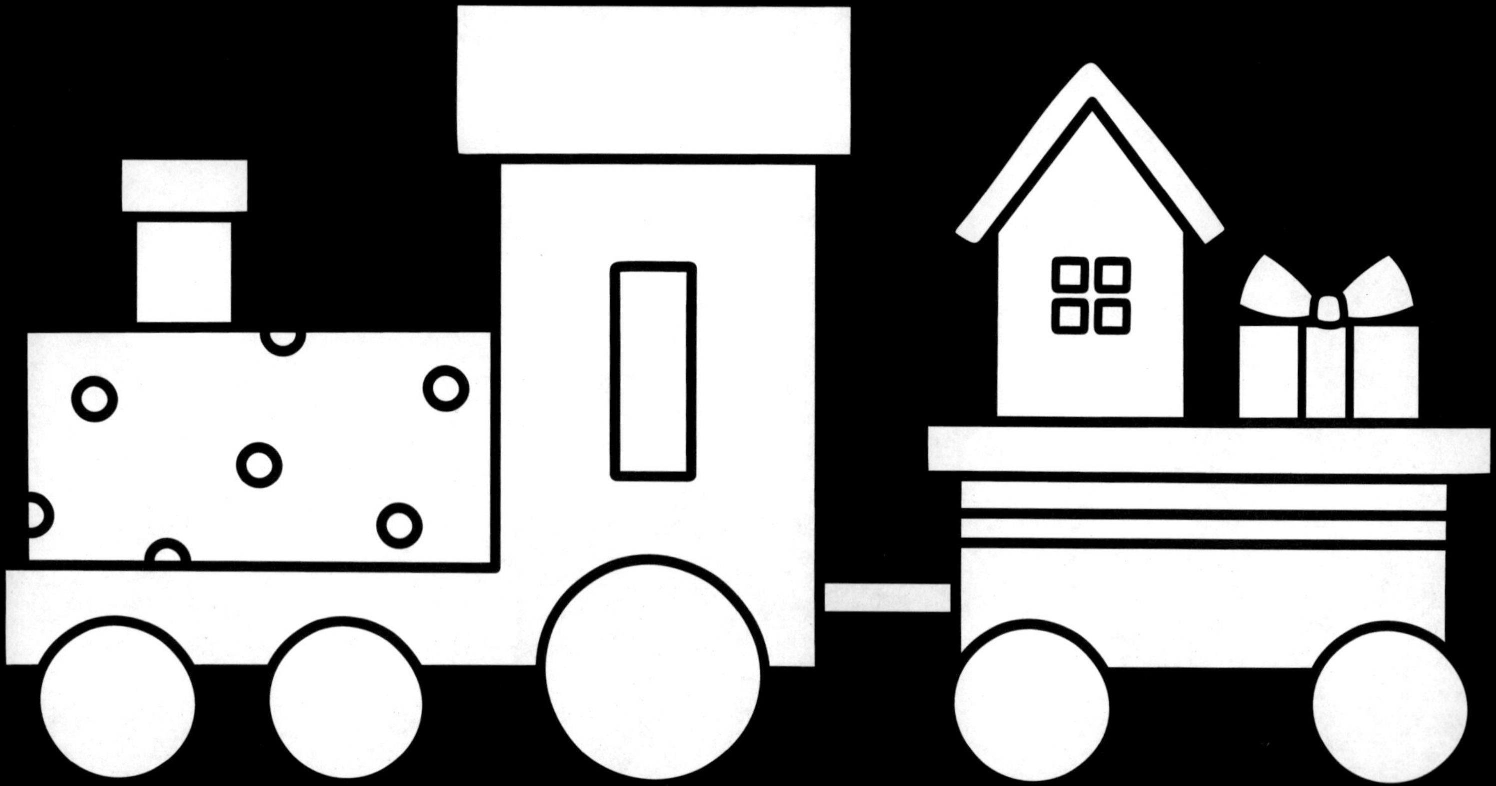

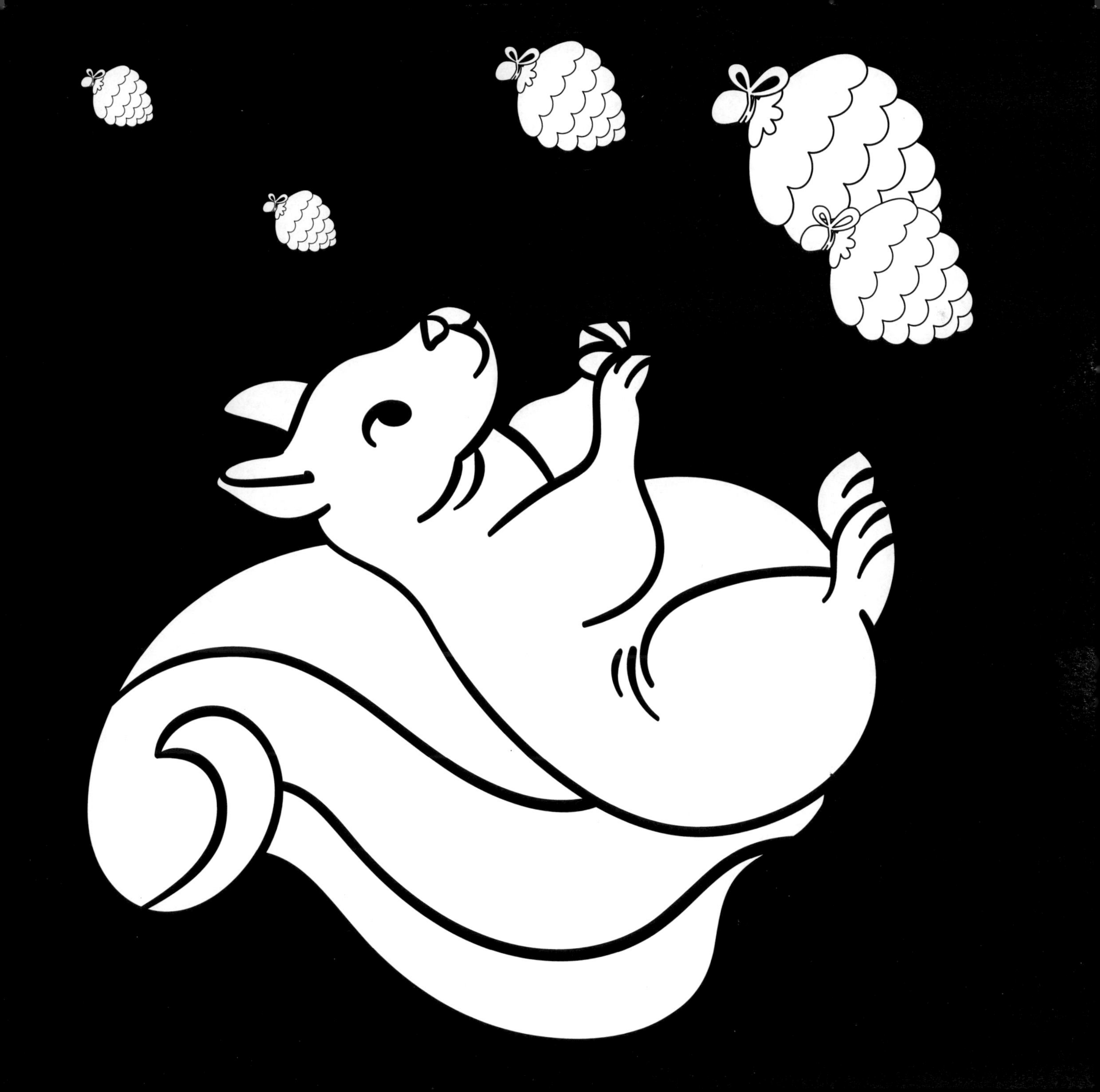

Manufactured by Amazon.ca
Acheson, AB

31990726R00017